How to Be a Good Leader

The Ultimate Guide to Developing the Managerial Skills, Teamwork Skills, and Good Communication Skills of an Effective Leader

by Terry Cochran

Table of Contents

Introduction 1

Chapter I: Discover Your Leadership Style and Personality 7

Chapter II: Show Your Expertise 15

Chapter III: Taking Your Listening Skills to the Next Level 19

Chapter IV: Motivate Your Followers 25

Conclusion 29

Introduction

As the human race has evolved, it has been socially dependent on certain members deemed leaders of the group. These particular people always possessed characteristics that a group of people could rally around in order to reach their goals. Even in the animal kingdom, wild animals will gather around a dominant animal to lead them. For example, a pride of lions has one king lion that leads the pack and ensures every lion is properly fed and protected. Because the male lion will fight to the death for the top spot, this ensures the king is the strongest and therefore the most able to protect and hunt food for his pride, or group.

Of course, in today's civilized world, we don't exactly have to fight to the death to lead a group of people. But, in a manner of speaking, any potential leader does have to fight or compete to obtain a leadership position. Instead of proving strength and power, the candidate will have to display how and why they're the most suitable for the position. Instead of physically lunging at an opponent, the candidate is required to constantly demonstrate professional and social skills a cut above the rest. Both of these skills are key leaderships characteristics. A leader could be outstanding at what they do, but if they don't know how to deal with people, they will not make the cut. Similarly, a person could have exceptional people skills, able to inspire and motivate, but if they don't really have the knowledge to back it up they won't get far on the leadership track.

The traits that make an effective leader are very similar throughout a wide span of fields and types of organizations. One desirable trait is the ability to keep your mind open, and a willingness to grow and learn. A good leader won't necessarily know how to do everything, but they are willing to take the initiative to learn helpful skills. Another leadership trait is a strong work ethic, able and willing to work harder than the average person. This trait is important to ensure that everyone in the group is working hard in each role, and the best way to do that is to lead by example.

Natural leaders are also creative and highly effective motivators. As stated earlier, one way they inspire and excite others is by their hard-work. Words can definitely be motivating, but nothing speaks quite so loudly as actions. Yet, strong leaders are often misunderstood and sometimes unfairly judged. Therefore, it's necessary for a leader to build a thick skin and focus on the task at hand. They have to ignore unfair comments and put energy into helping their group work hard to reach their goals. Keep your eye on the prize, as they say. Often it is a person's 'differences' that get them to a leadership position. They're effective at communicating, and aren't shy to network and meet new people. And with being a good communicator, comes the skill of being a good listener. A strong leader will rise above the noise, and both listen as well as hold a commanding voice.

This book will help you to develop all the attributes that define a great leader, and will help you discover how to use those qualities to bring your career and personal life to new heights.

Chapter I: Discover Your Leadership Style and Personality

No two persons are the same – not even twins. We are each unique beings, every person having physical, emotional and mental traits unlike anyone else. The reason behind this is to ensure variety in the human race, helping the species propagate (grow and spread). Imagine that all humans look and think alike, with the same exact interests. Everyone would strive for the same goal, same position in the group. A group is like any 'machine; and needs all the different parts to work properly as a whole. You can't have a group made up entirely of leaders or with all followers doing the same task. Each unique person plays an important and different role to keep a group working well. Thus, variety is a very good, healthy thing.

Everyone interacts in different ways to other people, based on their unique personality and style. Psychologists group different types of personalities into categories, though these categories/groupings vary from one school of thought to the next. Each school of thought focuses on/looks at different facets of the personality. These facets include consciousness, attitude, psychology, etc. Carl Jung's model for personality typing is the one most used today. In terms of attitude, Jung sees people can be one of two types: extroverted, or introverted. People who are extroverted get energy from interacting with people – socializing. Introverts gain their energy from being alone. Their energy gets used up quickly during social interactions, requiring them to get more 'alone time' to reboot/reenergize. Extroverts like to be on the edge, and often take risks, while introverts prefer to think before they act, being more careful and cautious.

It is helpful for a leader to know which personality type they have as this can affect how they lead. An extrovert tends to be more widely liked than an introvert since they are more naturally suited to social situations. These people make great motivators and leaders, attracting a large, avid group of followers. That's not to say an introverted person cannot be a good leader. Though not always as popular, introverts tend to be smarter leaders that make better decisions. Introverts are some of the brightest, most successful people in the world because they take the time, on their own without other people distracting, to think carefully through each decision before acting on it.

Don't let this information influence you either way. Your personality type doesn't ultimately affect your ability to be a strong leader. Many people assume that being introverted means you're shy, but that is not necessarily true. You may need to gain energy from being alone, but then you can use that energy to be vibrant and social in public. It's just that the introverts may need more time out of the public eye to be that energized social person. In any case, whether you're an extrovert or an introvert, you have the potential to be a strong, motivating leader.

We have talked about the different personality types and how those relate to leadership. Now let's take a look at different leadership styles that tend to go along with each personality type.

1. Authoritarian Leader

Authoritarian leaders, also sometimes referred to as autocratic leaders, like the name implies, have total authority over how their group of followers act and operate in the society or organization. Strict regulations, policies, or laws are enforced so that it is clear to the group what must be done, or avoided, in order to obey. Authoritarian leaders also tend to have a strictly professional or business relationship with their group, creating a distinct and absolute line between leader and follower. They don't want to be perceived as a 'friend' or an equal, simply a ruler to follow without question.

Authoritarians will have managers and supervisors under them in order to maintain a successful rule. These managers keep a close eye on the group, overseeing completion of necessary work and adhering to rules. Authoritarian leaders feel that this is the only way to get work done and keep order. Examples of countries are ruled by this style of leadership are Cuba and North Korea. While this style can benefit those who work best under constant supervision, this type of environment becomes confining for creative people or anyone who wants to do things in an unconventional way.

2. Democratic Leader

Unlike authoritarians, this style of leader doesn't rely solely on their own decision-making abilities, but depend on help from the group. Democratic leaders will debate with their followers, as well as discuss new ideas to encourage more involvement. Even though democrats prefer group input, it isn't a 'free-for-all' style. It's group-oriented, but not chaotic. The leader still sets certain guidelines which the group must adhere to.

Some people may not fully understand this kind of leader, thinking they're foolish to put any of their power into the group. However, research shows that the democratic style of leadership is often the most effective and productive.

3. Leader as Equal

In this style of leadership, the leader actually tends to shy away from supervising the group, believing that everyone will be happier, and thus perform better, when left to take responsibility for themselves and their own tasks. Decisions are made as a group, as if everyone is equal. This style of leadership usually applies to leaders who work with people just as experienced as themselves, therefore not requiring much supervision. If this type of leadership is applied to groups with less experience and motivation, then it could result in non-cohesiveness, lack of productivity and general dissatisfaction.

4. Reward-based Leader

This type of leader motivates the group of followers using a reward and/or punishment system to boost the quality of work. Rewards can be tangible or psychological, given for good performance and sometimes for a good show of effort. A tangible reward could something monetary like a bonus or a raise. A psychological reward could be something like 'employee of the month' or a name in the hall of fame. If anybody doesn't meet the expectations, they are given corrective measures to improve performance. This type of leader is great for an organization that is trying to mature and be more productive in order to reach its goals.

5. Leader by Influence

These leaders attempt to influence the outlook of the group, through finding ways to inspire them with a sense of purpose. This type of leader doesn't care how they're viewed by the group. They simply have passionate ambitions and vision, and strongly persist in sharing this with the group. However, they don't think of the group as sheep that will follow them blindly. Instead, they want to challenge everyone to think deeply and independently. It's not hard for a member of the group to be able to meet directly with the leader because they remain highly available and visible in the organization.

Every leader falls into one of these five types of leadership style. Some may appear more effective and kinder than others, but every type has its pros and cons. None of them are perfect, but they can all operate effectively in some situation.

Chapter II: Show Your Expertise

The blind do not want to be led by another blind person. If people are to follow you, they will have to know that you can do what you say you can. To ascend to a leadership position, you must have an expertise of some kind that sets you apart from the rest of the candidates for a position. If you want to be a leader in a specific field, say football, or pharmaceuticals, your knowledge and experience in the field needs to go above and beyond others in the field. Now, a leader need not know absolutely every minute detail of an organization, in fact many leaders know maybe 50% of everything. What they need to know are the most important things, or the aspects that they can specialize in.

Take a business like IBM that does just about everything computer-related.   The employee from the Servers department rising through the ranks will not know every tiny detail about IBM like ATMs, security software, and so on. Yet, they will know servers inside and out, and have the uncanny ability to motivate those around them. They will more likely be chosen for CEO before a "jack of all trades". So if you strive to be a leader in any organization, it is beneficial to know a specific skill inside and out, rather than all facts of the organizations history. Know your area of expertise and stick to it.

If you have expertise in a certain field, don't be afraid to develop on top of that. Be confident in your knowledge and be sure to let others see and know how talented you are. You could be the most skilled person in your department, but if you lack confidence people will find it hard to realize your potential. If you muster up the confidence to let people know of your expertise, you have a better chance of moving upwards. On top of allowing your expertise to show, it's important to then take initiative to get the attention of the leaders. When people in the leadership group notice your hard work and expertise, they will give you increasingly important tasks, and want you to help and supervise those around you. This is how promotion happens.

In order to get people to notice your skills, networking is the way to go. One excellent way to network in general is to join a good-will society such as the Kiwanis Club. Also, you can join a group that has exhibits your specific skills. If you are a great singer, then think about joining a choir or band. Likewise, if you have an outstanding jump shot, find a neighborhood pick-up game of basketball. These little things will help you to get noticed. You could also try a society or organization in your specific field, one that may charge a fee but is also may have competitions, workshops or meetings that involve leaders in that field. While it might be expensive, the networking and door-opening you could get is invaluable. Of course, there are free sites for social networking such as Facebook and Twitter. However, if you want to make an impression in the professional community, then you should try LinkedIn or similar.

After joining the social organization of your choice, then you can take even more initiative by volunteering to speak at various engagements and functions. Say you're good at making and investing money, then you could volunteer to speak at a finance and commerce seminar. Universities are also a great place to start. You can give a guest lecture for a class in your field or give a public lecture related to your area of expertise. This may be challenging for those of you not so great at public speaking, but you can view it as practice for your future leadership role. It can be helpful to use material online or at the library that offers useful tips on public speaking.

Once you feel you've gained a solid amount of knowledge and experience in your field, consider writing a book in that field. And, if the thought of book writing is too overwhelming, then you can start and maintain a blog in your chosen field. This is easier and often even more effective at reaching a wide audience. If you put up interesting, well-written posts, you blog could gain high traffic. And the more traffic, or the more popular, the more potential you have of getting noticed by someone in a powerful leadership position. Someone who could have the ability to offer you a position of higher leadership in your field. Now, if writing isn't your forte, you can try posting your expertise using YouTube videos or podcasts instead. They can all get you the attention you need to rise up in your field.

Chapter III: Taking Your Listening Skills to the Next Level

One of the most important qualities for any person to have is the ability to listen. People feel comforted, empowered and worthwhile when someone truly listens to them. In terms of being an effective leader, listening helps you to gain insight into the opinions, views and feelings of others. Everyone has their own particular, potentially helpful point-of-view. When a leader knows how their followers differ, they can use that knowledge to put together a varied team that works effectively together. Listening also comes in handy when the inevitable disagreements occur within the group. As a leader, it will be your responsibility to ensure that each party has a fair chance in explaining their view on the issue. These situations can get emotional and difficult to mediate, thus requiring a fair and understanding listening ability to resolve the dispute.

Another useful aspect of strong listening skills is to gain helpful viewpoints that may differ from your own. It can be hard, at first, to train your mind to be more open to hear different ideas and opinions, but its' worth it. The ability to view life and the world through someone else's eyes is one of the key skills for a good listener. People have different perspective on things, and often you will find that there is not just one right one over the others. Each individual's perspective has value and could help lead to an innovative idea or a smart decision – maybe one you wouldn't have thought up on your own.

Another quality of a good listener is to always maintain eye contact. Some say you listen first and foremost with your eyes, then your ears. We communicate a lot with our eyes, and by just looking at a person's eyes and face we can tell their emotional state. Good eye contact helps you to "hear" the things that are left unsaid by the person. You can also express emotions using your eyes in order for the person to know you understand what they're saying. Keeping your eyes open will also indicate that you are genuinely listening to every word. Depending on what personality type you are, extrovert or introvert, this leadership quality may be more or less difficult. Listening is also important in every leadership style. Even an authoritarian who rules with an iron fist benefits from good listening. People who listen are more observant and can often make the best, most informed decisions.

One common mistake people make while listening is to compare the other person to themselves. This can be problematic. Everyone experiences life in their own way. Even if you have experienced something they are going through now, keep it to yourself and continue listening. The less "I" and the more "you", the better. The person who is doing the talking doesn't really want to hear much about your experiences while they're expressing their own. They are more looking for insight into what to do or simply a sympathetic, understanding ear. The only time it is recommended to talk about how you tackled a situation is if they ask for it. But, if this situation arises, never make it seem you have experienced the same thing that the person has. Know that your experiences are similar, but never exactly the same.

Learn how to sympathize and give indications that you are listening. You could do that by giving the occasional nod, or "mhmm", or anything in the affirmative. Looking in their eyes is often not enough on its own – you could maintain excellent eye contact while your mind is elsewhere. Adding other things like, "okay," and "I see," along with the eye contact will show even more that you are truly listening. You have to interject those words or phrases at the right time though, as you don't want to accidentally say something inappropriate or appear like your interrupting too much.

During each conversation, keep note of all the key points of what a person's saying. Restating something that was said earlier when you are giving feedback will tell the person that you really were listening to them, and they will then want to tell you more. We're not saying you have to remember word-for-word what the person said, simply noting one key point within a five minute timeframe will work. When you do this, you will be able to follow-up with the person even days or weeks after the conversation ended. Following up is also a very important ability for a leader.

The final thing to hone your listening skills is - know what to say and when to say it. Don't try to talk too soon, as you will need to silently listen first before you speak. In some cases, you might not need to say anything at all. Like when a person shares something emotional and personal, you should look sympathetic and reassure them of your confidentiality. A good listener is also one that can keep things to themselves when appropriate. If it is appropriate to speak after the person is finished, and wants feedback, try to recall all the main points of the conversation, and restate them along with your feedback on each point.

Chapter IV: Motivate Your Followers

Whether it's through a mantra, or through their own hard work and determination, a great leader possesses the knack of motivating everyone around them to achieve their fullest potential. People often contradict themselves - they say they want to achieve certain things, such as lose weight, or get financially secure by a certain age, but end up not doing so because of one thing: lack of motivation. Motivation comes in many forms. What motivates you may not motivate another, and vice versa. Whatever inspires and motivates a person is unique to them. So motivating not only yourself, but a group of people takes an extraordinary amount of skill and determination. Some are born with the natural ability to motivate, while others need to learn it. Luckily, you can take certain steps, along with practice, to obtain the ability to motivate.

To begin on your path in becoming a great motivator, you must learn to "generate and sustain trust," according to scholar Warren Bennis. A great motivator doesn't just verbally express the way in which their followers must go, but instead shows the way through their own action. Great motivators model the way in which the group must go by personal example and dedication. As they say, actions speak louder than words.

Motivational leaders will also have a highly knowledgeable group of people surrounding them. As stated earlier, a leader may not know every single detail about their organization, but they will surround themselves with highly competent people that can work effectively with minimal management. Even though a leader may hire people with more detailed knowledge than they have, the leader exudes the confidence required to manage and lead them.

Motivators are highly visionary people. And they have the ability to communicate their vision in an exciting manner, inspiring all who hear it. Not only do they recognize their own dreams, but they recognize the dreams and visions of the group as a whole. The leader takes the dreams of each individual and incorporates it into the goal of the entire organization. The leader and group will then work together to foster and nurture those collective dreams until they become reality.

Be humble. That's one of the most important aspects of being a great motivator. No matter how far up the top you get, always take those with a lower position seriously. Always listen to those around you, as most times you will learn something useful and beneficial for the organization. A strong motivator is also great at getting inspiring others to take action.

Other key qualities in becoming a strong motivator are patience, creativity, confidence, and flexibility. Motivational leaders are also courageous. Remember, being courageous doesn't mean you don't have any fears. Courageous people sometimes have the worst fears, they simply respond to fear differently. Being courageous means that you are willing to take risks to tackle problems, regardless of your fear.

If you have self-esteem issues, as many people do, try and improve your esteem. If you feel bad about yourself and your worth, then others won't look to you as a condiment, leading role model, making it difficult to motivate them. Some researchers say that the way you feel about yourself is the basis for all motivated behavior. A great motivator will not only work on their own esteem, but work on the esteem of others around them. This can be done by raising the follower's awareness of themselves and their value in helping the organization. The motivational leader can help any individual in the group with low self-esteem or other issues combat any negative thoughts and replace them with positive, worthwhile ones.

Conclusion

People can be categorized into two types in the business world - the leaders and the followers. Not everyone is meant to be a leader, and that's okay. It is better for one person to lead a group of ten people, than a group of ten people to lead one. We listed some of the main attributes in an effective leader. Every leader is different in their own way, varying in personality and intellect among other things. If you believe you are leadership material, don't think you need to be exactly like Steve Jobs or something to lead your group to success. Know that he was only one type of leader, and that others, like Tim Cook, can fill his position effectively, even though he has a different managerial style. Everyone operates differently, and the only way to really be effective at what you do is to realize and embrace that difference.

Throughout this book, we discussed mainly leadership and not managerial styles. While these often go hand-in-hand, they are not exactly the same. However, they possess similarities since to be a good manager you need to be a good leader. The difference is that a leader is often the person making final decisions and ideas that get passed along to the managers who, in turn, manages carrying those ideas and decisions out. This book deals specifically with the 'top dog' of an organization, the leader.

People do not want someone to just deal out tasks and designate work. What people want more is a leader that can inspire a sense of purpose and excitement about the task-at-hand. So even if you don't become the CEO, President or

Vice-President of your organization, you can still be a great manager not only by assigning tasks, but by leading them into a passionate, exciting, motivated attitude toward work and the dreams of the organization.

Finally, I'd like to thank you for purchasing this book! If you enjoyed it or found it helpful, I'd greatly appreciate it if you'd take a moment to leave a review on Amazon. Thank you!

Printed in Great Britain
by Amazon

13011603R00020